1OO

FACTS

EVERTON

FACTS

EVERTON

Bob Sharp

WYMER
WP
PUBLISHING
Bedford, England

First published in Great Britain in 2018
by Wymer Publishing
www.wymerpublishing.co.uk
Wymer Publishing is a trading name of Wymer (UK) Ltd

ISBN 978-1-908724-12-0

Edited by Jerry Bloom.

Typeset by The Andys.
Printed and bound in Great Britain by Clays Ltd, Elcograf S.p.A.

A catalogue record for this book is available from the British Library.

Cover design by The Andys.
Sketches by Becky Welton. © 2014.

1878
ST
DOMINGO'S

Everton Football Club was formed in 1878 and
initially named St Domingo's.

St Domingo's Church stood at the corner of
Breckfield Road North and St Domingo Vale. The
minister was the Reverend Ben Swift Chambers
who had first formed a cricket team for members
of a bible class. However as this was only played in
summer, a sport for the winter was required and
they chose association football.

The first St Domingo's game to be reported
in the press was against Everton Church Club on
a pitch that was barely marked at the southeast
corner of Stanley Park. The players had to carry
the goalposts themselves from a park lodge and
in what was described in the press as a closely
contested game, St Domingo's won 1-0. They soon
developed a reputation as the best team that played
matches in Stanley Park.

St Domingo's Church was demolished in
1972 and the site is now sheltered flats. Ben Swift
Chambers died in 1901 and for many years his grave
lay neglected in a churchyard in the Yorkshire
village of Shepley. However in 2008 it was restored
with help being given by the club.

As St Domingo's FC developed they soon outgrew the church and members took the decision to change the name to Everton.

The meeting that led to the name change took place in the Queens Hotel in Village Street. Six members were present and the name was changed to reflect the fact that more players who didn't attend St Domingo's were turning out for the club. The name Everton was chosen as it was the district in which the church was situated.

On 20th December 1879 the first match took place under the name of Everton. Wearing blue and white striped shirts, Everton beat St Peter's 6-0 at Stanley Park although there is no record of the line-ups or scorers. There were only a handful of spectators and they were not required to pay any entrance fee. A month later the clubs played a return fixture, with Everton winning 4-0.

One of those who watched with interest in those early days was local brewer and councillor John Houlding, whose house overlooked Stanley Park. He would go on to play a major part in the history of Everton over the next thirteen years.

1883
PRIORY
ROAD

Everton moved to a new home in 1883 but they would remain there for only one season.

Crowds at Stanley Park were now exceeding 2,000 and spectators were regularly encroaching onto the pitch. By renting a gated enclosure on Priory Road, the club could now charge admission fees and keep those attending under control.

The first game there was on 27th October between representative sides from the football associations of Liverpool and Walsall. Spectators wishing to attend were advised in the press to take the tram to Cabbage Hall or horse drawn omnibus to Arkles Lane.

Everton remained at the ground for just one season, playing friendlies and Liverpool Senior Cup games. Noise from spectators has often been documented as the reason for them having to leave the ground, although further research in recent years has suggested this may not be the case.

The ground was well away from any houses and unlikely to have been a disturbance to anybody. Its location though did make it difficult to access and it could well have been that it was simply too far for spectators to travel and then have to pay an admission fee. It meant Everton were on the move again, this time to Anfield Road.

1884
ANFIELD
ROAD

With Everton needing a ground that was more easily accessible, their main backer John Houlding found the perfect solution when he arranged rental of a field near his hotel.

Houlding owned the Sandon Hotel on Oakfield Road. Along with another brewer named John Orell he also part owned a nearby field on Anfield Road. Houlding acted as an agent for Orrell and set up a lease of the field, with the Sandon becoming the club's headquarters.

Fencing and hoarding were erected, with the first game taking place on 28th September 1884. Everton beat Earlestown 5-0 in a game that was watched by 1,000 spectators.

During that first season Everton's gate revenue quadrupled. Over the next eight seasons, Anfield was developed into an enclosure capable of holding 20,000 spectators and was even selected by the Football Association for an international with Ireland in 1889.

Everton's tenure at Anfield was at first a happy one but after the formation of the Football League in 1888 relations with Houlding and Orell became strained. This led to the club moving again in 1892, to the land that became Goodison Park.

1884
LIVERPOOL SENIOR
CUP WINNERS

Everton won their first trophy in 1884 when they triumphed in the final of the Liverpool Senior Cup.

Everton reached the final thanks to victories over St. Peters, Ramblers and Bootle Wanderers. Their opponents were Earlestown, who had knocked out the previous year's winners, Bootle. The final was played at Hawthorne Road in Bootle on 29th March and was attended by 2,500 spectators. This included 500 who had come from Earlestown on a special excursion train.

Everton dominated the first half but were let down by some poor shooting by their forwards. After the break the game was more even but midway through the half they got the decisive goal. Edwin Berry crossed from the left and there was a scrimmage, leading to the ball breaking loose and William Parry firing home. The Earlstown players' appeals for offside were rejected by the referee.

Everton had to wait until the Annual General Meeting of the Liverpool FA in June to be presented with the trophy, which was then displayed at the Sandon Hotel.

1887
FA CUP
DISQUALIFICATION

Everton's first tie in the FA Cup was a marathon one involving four games and eventual disqualification.

After being drawn away to Bolton Wanderers in the first round, Everton lost 1-0 on 15th October. However as Bolton fielded an ineligible player the FA ordered a replay, which took place two weeks later at Anfield. Everton scored a last minute equaliser to make it 2-2 and force extra time, during which there was no further scoring.

On 12th November the two sides met at Burnden Park and this time the game ended in a 1-1 draw. Everton led at the break but Bolton levelled with ten minutes to go and as it was too dark extra time couldn't be played. The following week the tie eventually appeared to be settled when Everton won 2-1 at Anfield.

Everton went on to face Preston North End in the next round and lost 6-0. However there was a further twist when Bolton successfully appealed that Everton had fielded seven ineligible players in their first round victory. The FA reinstated Bolton into the competition and they faced Preston themselves, only to lose 9-0.

1890
RECORD
VICTORY

Everton's record victory was on 18th January 1890, when three players scored hat-tricks as they thrashed Derby County 11-2 in an FA Cup first round tie at Anfield.

In an evenly matched first half Fred Geary opened the scoring for Everton but John Goodall scored twice to put the visitors ahead. As halftime approached Geary equalised and then set up Alf Milward to put Everton 3-2 ahead at the break.

After the restart Everton extended their lead thanks to long-range efforts from Alexander Brady and David Kirkwood. Brady then scored another from a free kick and completed his hat-trick to take the score to 7-2. Alf Milward headed the eighth and Daniel Doyle got the ninth with a fine solo run and shot.

The tenth goal was a header by Geary and the eleventh came from Milward. Derby had been hopelessly overrun in the second half, having little stamina to compete on an extremely muddy pitch. The margin of victory was a surprise considering both clubs were in the Football League, Derby finishing that season in seventh while Everton were second.

Everton couldn't build on this victory and were knocked out in the next round, losing 4-2 at Stoke.

1891
THE FIRST CHAMPIONSHIP MEDALS

When Everton won the Football League Championship for the first time in 1890-91, their players were the first to receive medals for their achievement.

Everton had a great start to the season, winning their first five games and scoring 23 goals. Three straight defeats curtailed them in November but they then regained consistency, winning eight out of their next ten.

By the end of January Everton had completed all bar one of their fixtures and had established quite a lead at the top. They then looked on nervously as Preston closed the gap to just two points with one game each remaining.

On 14th March Everton needed just a draw at Burnley to be confirmed as champions and 800 fans travelled on a special excursion train. They lost 3-2, but still triumphed as Preston lost 3-0 at Sunderland.

A consistent line-up had been a key to Everton's success. Seven players appeared in twenty or more of the 22 fixtures. Striker Fred Geary was an ever present and contributed with twenty goals.

Although Everton would later be presented with the championship trophy, there was no provision for players to receive individual awards. Everton's directors decided to have medals cast for the squad. The following year the Football League adopted this idea and it has been in operation ever since.

1892
THE FIRST PURPOSE BUILT
FOOTBALL GROUND

Everton developed the first purpose built football ground in the world when they left Anfield after falling out with John Houlding.

A dispute over rent payments led to Everton members voting to leave Anfield. John Houlding formed Liverpool FC while Everton chairman George Mahon arranged a move to a piece of land called Mere Green, on other side of Stanley Park.

The new ground was named Goodison Park, after the road it ran alongside. Three new stands were constructed and the first game there took place on 2nd September, when Everton beat Bolton Wanderers 4-2 in a friendly.

On the same day that Goodison Park opened, Celtic Park in Glasgow also hosted its first football match. Everton can claim to have had the first purpose built football ground in the world though, as Celtic's also had cycle and running tracks.

One publication, *Out of Doors*, reported that Goodison was 'One of the finest and most complete grounds in the Kingdom'. Everton could now attract crowds of up to 30,000 which was considered huge at the time.

During its time Goodison has hosted England internationals, FA Cup finals and semi-finals, and World Cup fixtures. It is now known as The Grand Old Lady by many fans, but changing times have made it unsuitable for modern spectator demands.

1893
FA CUP FINAL
REPLAY REFUSED

Everton's first appearance in the FA Cup final was in 1893, when they lost 1-0 to Wolverhampton Wanderers. Everton were unhappy about the playing environment but their request for the game to be replayed was refused.

Everton reached the final by beating West Bromwich Albion, Nottingham Forest, Sheffield Wednesday and Preston. They were favourites to beat Wolves in the final, which was played at Fallowfield in Manchester.

The official attendance was 45,000 but it was estimated to be nearer to 60,000, far more than the stadium was designed to hold. Spectators were encroaching onto the pitch making wing play impossible, leading to both sides playing long balls down the middle.

It was goalless at halftime but Wolves took the lead after an hour when Harry Allen's lob deceived the keeper. Everton protested that they hadn't been able to clear the ball properly due to the crowd and that Allen should never have had the opportunity.

Everton tired and couldn't get back into the game and after the final whistle there was a pitch invasion by Wolves supporters. Everton protested to the FA that competitive football was not possible in the environment and asked for a replay, but this was rejected. However, Fallowfield was never used for a final again.

1893
JACK SOUTHWORTH
SCORES SIX

The only Everton player to score six goals in one game was Jack Southworth against West Bromwich Albion on 30th December 1893.

Southworth joined from Blackburn Rovers at the start of the season, scoring his first goal in a 7-3 defeat at Derby County on 9th September.

At Goodison Park on 30th December John Bell scored Everton's opening goal against Albion, but after that Southworth took over. His first goal was from a header and the next two came about after Albion's keeper rushed out and completely missed the ball, allowing him to score with ease.

It was 4-0 at halftime and Everton then had the advantage of the wind after the break. Southworth got his fourth soon after the restart before Albion pulled a goal back. Southworth then got two in quick succession to complete a double hat-trick. He could have added to his tally, but he had another effort ruled out for offside and also hit the post as the game finished 7-1.

This victory came just a week after Everton had thrashed Sheffield Wednesday 8-0, a game in which Southworth netted four. He finished the season as the Football League's top scorer with 27 goals. However the following season injury forced him to retire and he became a professional violinist with the Halle Orchestra.

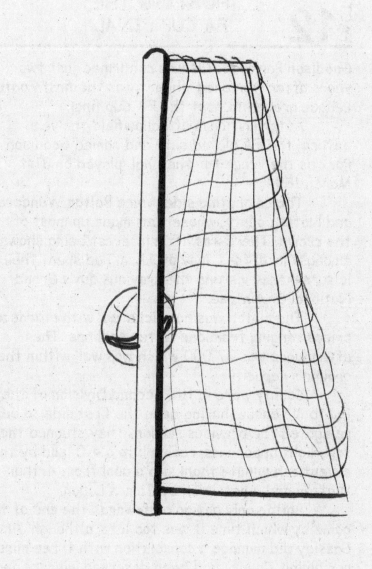

1894
HOSTING THE
FA CUP FINAL

Goodison Park's status was confirmed just two years after it opened when it was the first Football League ground to host the FA Cup final.

After criticism of Fallowfield the year before, the FA played safe and named Goodison Park as the venue for the final, played on 31st March 1894.

The competing sides were Bolton Wanderers and Notts County, whose fans made up most of the crowd. There was little interest being shown amongst local fans, may of whom had spent their leisure money visiting the previous day's Grand National at Aintree.

The match was not ticketed, with entrance prices ranging from one to ten shillings. The attendance was 37,000 which was well within the ground's capacity.

County were in the Second Division of the Football League, having been the first side to be relegated the previous season. They stunned their top-flight opponents, racing into a 4-0 lead by the seventieth minute thanks to a goal from Arthur Watson and a hat-trick by James Logan.

Bolton only got going towards the end of the game by which time it was too late, although Jim Cassidy did manage a consolation with three minutes remaining. County had been deserved winners and belied their Second Division status.

1894
SILK HATS FOR
WINNING DERBY

In the very first Merseyside derby Everton beat Liverpool 3-0 on 13th October 1894, after which each player was awarded the bonus of a silk hat.

After their formation in 1892 Liverpool won the Lancashire League. They were then elected to the Football League Second Division, winning promotion in their first season to join Everton in the top flight.

For the first meeting between the teams at Goodison Park Everton underwent rigid coaching at their ground while Liverpool spent a week preparing in Hightown. There was a huge interest in the match, with the Lord Mayor being amongst the 44,000 crowd.

Tom McInnes gave Everton the lead after ten minutes when he reacted first to a Billy Stewart free kick. McInnes then set up Alex Latta for the second goal after an hour. With two minutes remaining John Bell's deflected shot made it 3-0.

The club minute books recorded that each player was given a bonus of a silk hat worth £1 for winning the game. This was a substantial reward given the players' wages at the time were no more than £4. The following month Everton returned to Anfield for the first time since the split and looked set for victory, until a late penalty allowed Liverpool to snatch a 2-2 draw.

1897
CUP FINAL DEFEAT TO
DOUBLE WINNERS

Everton reached their second FA Cup final in 1897, but they were beaten by Aston Villa who did the double of Football League Championship and FA Cup that season.

Everton knocked out Burton Wanderers, Bury, Blackburn Rovers and Derby County to reach the final. They spent a few days preparing at Lytham before travelling to London on 9th April, the day before the game. They knew they would have a hard task against Villa, who were the runaway league leaders.

In front of a then English record crowd of 65,981 spectators at Crystal Palace, John Campbell's 25-yard strike gave Villa the lead after eighteen minutes. Five minutes after falling behind, Jack Bell equalised and then Jackie Boyle put Everton ahead before the half hour mark. Villa struck back though and equalised through Fred Wheldon. Jimmy Crabtree then headed them into a 3-2 lead just before halftime.

There were no further goals in the second half and after collecting the cup, Villa learned that they were also league champions due to other results having gone their way that day.

1901
ROYAL
BLUE

After sporting various colours for the first 23 years of their existence, Everton changed to royal blue in 1901. Except for one season, they have worn that colour ever since.

St Domingo's and then Everton started off in white shirts, followed by blue and white stripes. In those early days, new players would sometimes wear the shirts of their former clubs, causing all sorts of confusion on the pitch.

To ensure uniformity the club dyed all shirts black for a few years and in the first season at Goodison Park, Everton played in salmon pink and dark blue stripes. Later that decade they wore ruby with blue trimmings.

For the 1901-02 season, Everton adopted royal blue shirts with white shorts, which they wore for five seasons. When they briefly changed to sky blue in 1906 there were protests from fans and the shirts were quickly changed back.

There have been occasional seasons when Everton have worn a slightly lighter shade of blue. However changes have only ever been subtle and short lived, especially when the club are often referred to as 'The Blues'.

1905
THE FIRST
FOREIGN TOUR

Everton's first games outside of the British Isles were in May 1905 when they toured the Austro-Hungarian Empire.

The first game was against Magor Athekai (Hungarian Athletics Association) in Budapest on 1st May. The match was played in glorious sunshine and the Blues ran out 11-2 winners. They then travelled to Vienna and had no signs of fatigue as they beat First Vienna 4-0.

Five days later Everton came up against fellow tourists Tottenham Hotspur in Vienna. In front of a crowd of 8,000, the Blues won 2-0 and that evening a banquet was held in honour of both clubs. The next two games saw Everton beat Czech sides Sportclub Slavin 6-3 and Athletikkib 5-0.

The tour finished off with another game against Tottenham in Prague on 16th May, a goal from Fred Rouse being enough to give Everton a 1-0 victory.

The party travelled home via Berlin, where it was hoped to arrange a game but it didn't materialise. They arrived back in Liverpool on 20th May, telling reporters it had been an enjoyable experience although the pitches had been hard.

1906
THE FIRST
FA CUP

It was third time lucky when Everton reached the FA Cup final in 1906, as they finally got their hands on the trophy after two previous final defeats.

Everton knocked out Liverpool in the semi-final, beating their local rivals 2-0 at Villa Park. They were underdogs for the final against Newcastle United, the beaten finalists and league champions in 1905.

In front of over 75,000 fans at Crystal Palace the first half didn't live up to expectations. Apart from a Jimmy Settle header that was well saved by the Newcastle keeper, there were no other clear goal scoring opportunities as the sides battled it out in midfield.

In the second half Everton took control and thought they'd gone ahead in the 53rd minute when Sandy Young scored after the keeper dropped a cross, but it was ruled out for offside. Everton remained dominant and with thirteen minutes left the deadlock was finally broken. Jack Sharp crossed for Young, who made no mistake in firing the ball past the keeper. Everton held on for victory and were presented with the cup by Lord Kinnaird.

Two days later the team were met by huge crowds at Liverpool Central station, with mounted police escorting the players on a parade accompanied by the Lord Mayor and his carriage.

Everton reached the FA Cup final again in 1907, but despite being favourites they were unable to win the trophy for a second year running.

After early round wins over Sheffield United, West Ham, Bolton and Crystal Palace, Everton beat West Bromwich Albion 2-1 in the semi-final. Their opponents in the final at Crystal Palace on 20th April were The Wednesday, the name Sheffield Wednesday were known as until 1929.

The final was played on a glorious spring day but in the opening stages Everton failed to perform to their full potential. James Stewart deservedly put The Wednesday ahead after twenty minutes. Shortly before halftime Everton were level when Jack Sharp seized on a defensive error to hammer the ball into the net from twelve yards.

Everton were much better in the second half, with Young and Bolton both going close. However they were struggling to cope with Wednesday's physical approach and began to tire. A replay looked certain but with four minutes to go Simpson was left unmarked and headed in the winning goal for The Wednesday from two yards.

Despite finishing third in the table and ten points ahead of thirteenth place Wednesday, Everton had failed to become the first club in the 20th Century to retain the cup.

1909
EVERTON OF
CHILE

Everton's tour of South America in 1909 led to the formation of a club of the same name there, who eventually played their namesakes in a friendly.

The Everton party set off from Lime Street station on 13th May. They took a train to London then another to Southampton, before sailing to Buenos Aries via Lisbon, Madeira, Cape Verde, Rio de Janeiro and Montevideo. The exhausting journey took a total of 23 days.

Tottenham were also in South America and on 6th June the two sides faced each other in Buenos Aries and drew 2-2. Everton stayed in Buenos Aries and beat Alumni 3-0, then moved on to Montevideo where they beat a Uruguayan XI 2-1.

They then returned to Buenos Aries and played Tottenham again, winning 4-0 and completed their games on 20th June with a 4-1 victory over an Argentine League XI. Five days later the party boarded the steamer Asturals for the three-week journey home.

As Everton's players were preparing to sail home, an Englishman in Chile called David Foxley formed a club and named it in honour of the touring side. Everton de Vina del Mar, as they are now known, have won four national titles and travelled to Merseyside for a friendly in August 2010, with the Goodison Blues winning 2-0.

1910
JACK SHARP
RETIRES

Everton's multi talented captain Jack Sharp retired from playing in 1910, saying he wanted to go out at his peak.

Sharp was 22 years old when he joined Everton from Aston Villa in 1899. Playing as a winger, he played 300 league games over the next eleven seasons and scored 68 goals. Sharp was a member of the 1906 FA Cup winning side and scored in the following season's final defeat to The Wednesday.

Sharp was twice capped by England and he was also a professional cricketer. During the summer months he played for Lancashire, winning the County Championship in 1904. He also represented England at cricket, playing in a test series against Australia in 1909, scoring a century at The Oval.

At the end of the 1909-10 season Sharp announced his retirement from football. Even though he was Everton's captain, he said he wanted to leave at a time of his choosing and not be forced out.

Sharp continued to play cricket for Lancashire and also expanded his sports outfitter business in Liverpool city centre. His business supplied Everton's strip for many years and he was also a director at the club. His name lives on in Everton folklore and he is one of the club website's Millennium Giants.

1913
A ROYAL
VISIT

Goodison Park became the first football ground to be visited by a reigning monarch on 11th July 1913.

King George V was primarily on Merseyside to open the new Gladstone Dock. He then went to a reception at St George's Hall where the Lord Mayor, John Sutherland Harmood Banner, was knighted.

After a luncheon at the Town Hall the King and Queen Mary waved to crowds from the balcony. The royal carriage moved on to Goodison Park to watch a display given by 2,000 schoolchildren. Along with a crowd of 60,000 the royal couple watched synchronised dancing which including a movement that saw the children form into the shape of a Union flag.

Around 6pm the King and Queen left for Knowsley Hall, where they spent the night as guests of the Earl of Derby before undertaking further engagements in Manchester the following day.

104 years later George V's great grandson Prince Edward, Earl of Wessex opened the People's Hub in the shadow of Goodison Park. The building was developed as a home for the club charity Everton in the Community.

1915
WARTIME
CHAMPIONS

Everton won their second Football League Championship in 1914-15, the only time an English football season has been completed in wartime.

Britain declared war on Germany on 4th August 1914 but although cricket and rugby union suspended competition, football continued as normal.

After winning their opening two games, Everton lost three in succession. Things then clicked at the beginning of October with a 5-0 win over Liverpool at Anfield. Bobby Parker was the derby hero, scoring the first of six hat-tricks he would get during a season in which he scored 36 goals in 35 games.

Everton looked to have blown the title at Easter when they lost home games in successive days. They recovered by winning four in a row, meaning with one game left they led second placed Oldham on goal average.

The title was secured via the most unlikely source. On 24th April Liverpool won 2-0 at Oldham, meaning that Everton would be champions providing they didn't lose their last game 15-0.

On 26th April Everton completed their fixtures by twice coming from behind to draw 2-2 with Chelsea. The championship trophy was presented at the Football League's Annual General Meeting in July. The league was then suspended for the duration of the war and did not resume until 1919.

1918
WILL CUFF'S TEMPORARY RESIGNATION

Everton's successful secretary/manager Will Cuff resigned in 1918 as he was unable to combine both his football and business interests. He only managed to remain away from the game for three years however.

Born in 1868, Cuff got involved in Everton through St Domingo's Church and assisted with the move to Goodison Park in 1892. He became secretary in 1901, a role that involved recruiting players and selecting the team.

Under Cuff, Everton won both the Football League Championship and FA Cup. He had a great eye for spotting a youngster and helping them develop into a first team player, saving the club a fortune in transfer fees over the years.

Cuff combined his football duties with running his own legal practice. By 1918 this was expanding and he was unable to dedicate enough time to both roles, leading to him tendering his resignation.

Three years later Cuff was back at Everton when he was elected chairman. He oversaw two league title successes and another FA Cup, as well as the construction of the Bullens Road and Gwladys Street double-decker stands.

Cuff finally left Everton in 1938 when he became President of the Football League. He died in 1949 and is buried in Anfield Cemetery, where his headstone was restored in 2014 with help from the Everton Heritage Society.

1924
SAM CHEDGZOY'S CORNER KICK GOAL

A remarkable incident occurred in the game at Goodison Park on 15th November 1924. Sam Chedgzoy dribbled the ball from a corner kick and scored, leading to a change in the rules.

That summer there was a rule change that allowed goals to be scored direct from a corner and free kick. *Liverpool Echo* journalist Ernest Edwards spotted a loophole which did not prohibit the ball being dribbled.

After being told this by Edwards, Chedgzoy decided to try this when he was awarded a corner in the fixture with Arsenal. He placed the ball down, dribbled it and fired it into the goal. The referee came to have a word but Chedgzoy said he had done nothing wrong and after a quick consultation with the rulebook the goal was given.

Chedgzoy's goal didn't help Everton get a result in the game as they lost 3-2. Football officials had to act fast and quickly amended the wording of the rules. They were changed to state that once the player taking the corner had kicked the ball once, another had to touch it before he could do so again.

After finishing just one place outside the relegation zone in 1926-27, Everton won their third Football League Championship the following year with Dixie Dean's form being the prolific factor.

Dean joined Everton from Tranmere Rovers in 1925 and scored 32 goals in 38 games in his first full season. However in the summer of 1926 a serious motorbike crash led to him missing a number of games at the start of the next campaign.

Dean's absence was a major blow and Everton won just one of their first thirteen games with him out of the side. He eventually returned and scored 21 goals in 27 games as Everton finished twentieth, avoiding relegation by four points.

The following season it was all about Dean, who hit an incredible sixty goals, many of them thanks to the pinpoint crosses of Alec Troup. Highlights included all five in a 5-2 home win over Manchester United and a hat-trick in the Anfield derby which finished 3-3.

Everton were challenged by Leicester for much of the season but eventually it was Huddersfield who looked most likely to catch them. In the end, Huddersfield lost their penultimate game leaving Everton three points clear with a game to play. That meant the last day of the season it was all about helping Dean create a new record.

1928
SIXTY
LEAGUE GOALS

When Everton won the title in 1927-28 Dixie Dean scored an incredible sixty goals in 39 league games, a record that will surely never be beaten.

Dean scored in Everton's first nine games and his prolific goal scoring form continued throughout the season. On 28th April he scored four goals in a 5-3 win at Burnley that took the Blues to the brink of the title. Four days later closest challengers Huddersfield lost at Aston Villa, meaning Everton could not be caught at the top.

On 5th May a crowd of 48,715, the third highest at Goodison all season, turned out to see if Dean could now get the hat-trick he needed to reach sixty goals and surpass George Camsell, who had scored 59 for Middlesbrough the previous season.

Arsenal took an early lead but Dean quickly levelled. He then scored a sixth minute penalty to put Everton ahead but Arsenal did all they could to prevent him breaking the record, crowding him out at every opportunity.

With seven minutes to go Everton were awarded a corner and Dean rose to head the ball into the net. The cheers around the ground went on for several minutes and hardly anyone noticed when Arsenal made it 3-3. Dean had set a record that looks likely to remain forever.

1930
THE FIRST
RELEGATION

Just two years after they won the Football League Championship, Everton were relegated for the first time in their history in 1929-30.

Everton's main undoing was their form at Goodison Park, where they lost eight times. With five games left Everton's situation looked a hopeless one. They were bottom of the table and four points from safety, having won just three times since the turn of the year.

There was an improvement over Easter though and on Good Friday a crowd of 47,987 roared the Blues to a 3-0 victory over Burnley at Goodison Park. On Easter Saturday Everton drew 3-3 against Manchester United at Old Trafford, then a week later beat Sheffield United 3-2 at home.

The Blues then won 2-1 at Huddersfield in their penultimate game, but their rivals continued picking up points and their fate was still out of their hands.

On the final day of the season any two from four clubs could go down. Everton comfortably beat Sunderland 4-1 at Goodison Park but it was not enough, as victories for Newcastle and Sheffield United condemned the Blues to the drop.

Afterwards chairman Will Cuff tried to remain upbeat, telling the press that if the players showed as much fight as they had in the last few weeks they would soon be back in the First Division.

1931
GOALS GALORE ON
WAY TO PROMOTION

Will Cuff's prediction about a swift return to the top flight was correct, with Everton finishing as Second Division champions in 1930-31 to secure promotion, scoring 121 goals in 42 games.

The Blues started the season with five straight wins and they topped the table all season. There was no stopping Dixie Dean, who scored 39 goals in 37 games, with the rest being spread fairly evenly around the forward line.

Everton failed to score in only two league games and struck five or more goals on nine occasions. Charlton were beaten 7-1 at home and 7-0 away, while the biggest victory was a 9-1 mauling of Plymouth on 27th December 1930, the first of ten wins in succession.

Promotion and the title were secured with a 4-2 victory over Bradford at Goodison Park on 4th April in front of 32,213 fans. There were still five games remaining and although Everton only won one of them, they still finished seven points ahead of second place West Bromwich Albion.

At the last home game of the season on 18th April Everton were presented with the Championship Shield by John McKenna, President of the Football League. He described Everton's campaign as a 'homeward march'.

1932
CHAMPIONS A YEAR
AFTER PROMOTION

In 1931-32 Everton became only the second club to win the Football League Championship the season after being promoted.

The Blues won their first three games with Jimmy Dunn and Tommy White both getting hat-tricks. It took Dixie Dean six games to get off the mark but he did so in style, scoring all the goals in a 3-1 win over Liverpool at Anfield.

Dean had a devastating spell in the autumn, scoring twenty goals in ten games as Everton continued their devastating form in front of goal. He got five twice, in a 9-3 win over Sheffield Wednesday and 7-1 drubbing of Chelsea. There were also big wins over Leicester (9-2) and Newcastle (8-1).

In total Everton scored 116 goals, 84 of them at Goodison Park. Dean was the leading marksman with 45, but he was helped by Tommy Johnson who got 22 and White, who scored an impressive eighteen in 23 games.

Everton took a massive step towards the title on Good Friday with a 2-1 home win over close challengers West Bromwich Albion. They then held off competition from Arsenal and secured the title in the third from last game, when Dean scored the only goal in a 1-0 home win over Bolton.

1933
A MOMENTOUS FIRST
WEMBLEY APPEARANCE

Everton's first appearance at Wembley was in the 1933 FA Cup final, the first time numbered shirts were worn in a competitive match.

Going into the final against Manchester City, the press had mixed opinions on who was more likely to win. It was felt that Everton had the more skilful players, but City were a better physical team unit.

Both teams wore numbered shirts, with Everton wearing 1 to 11 and City 11 to 22. Neither side wore their home strip due to a colour clash, with Everton playing in white and City in red.

City started quickly, but Everton repelled their early attacks and soon took control. They didn't take the lead though until the 41st minute when Jimmy Stein scored from close range after the keeper had dropped a cross.

Seven minutes into the second half City's keeper again failed to hold the ball, allowing Dixie Dean to take full advantage and make it 2-0. Ten minutes from the end Jimmy Dunn converted Albert Geldard's cross to put the result beyond doubt.

Everton's players and fan partied long into the night. On arrival at Lime Street station, the players boarded a horse drawn carriage to parade the cup around the city centre.

1937
TOMMY
LAWTON

In January 1937 Everton paid what was then a record fee for a teenager. Tommy Lawton would replace Dixie Dean at centre forward but due to the outbreak of war he was unable to enjoy the same level of success.

Everton paid Burnley £6,500 for Lawton, whose seventeenth birthday had been only three months earlier. He scored four goals in eleven games before the end of the season and became a first choice starter for 1937-38.

Lawton scored 28 goals in 39 league games in his first full season at Everton. In 1938-39 when the Blues won the title, he found the net 34 times from 38 appearances. Like Dean, Lawton was good in the air but he also had great passing, dribbling and shooting ability.

The outbreak of World War Two brought Lawton's Everton career to an end. When peace resumed in 1945, he found it difficult to work with manager Theo Kelly and was also estranged from his wife who was in London.

Lawton was sold to Chelsea in November of that year, where he scored a club record 26 goals in 1946-47. He later played for Notts County, Brentford and Arsenal.

32

1938
THE
CREST

The first time Everton used the tower on its club crest was in 1938.

Since 1920 the club had been displaying a basic crest of EFC inside a shield on their shirts. In 1938 Theo Kelly was asked to design a crest that would be used on neckties. He thought about it for several months before coming up with the idea of using the building commonly known as 'The Beacon'.

The Beacon is actually named the Everton Lock-Up, Everton Tower, or Prince Rupert's Tower. It has stood on Everton Brow since 1787 and was used to lock up drunks. The ties were first worn by Kelly and chairman Ernest Green on the first day of the new season when Everton won 2-0 at Blackpool.

The crest wasn't used on the club shirts, which remained plain until the 1970s, when EFC was added. It was not until 1978 that a crest featuring the tower appeared on the shirts.

The lock-up features on a heritage trail in Everton Park and was restored in 1997 following a £15,000 donation from the club.

1939
TITLE WINNERS
DENIED GREATNESS

The Everton team that won the Football League Championship in 1938-39 was denied the chance to go on to greater things due to the outbreak of World War Two.

The Blues started the season with six straight wins and won eight of their first ten games. However a 3-0 defeat at Leicester in the last match of October saw them concede top spot to Derby County who remained there for three months.

On 4th February 1939 Everton beat Liverpool 3-0 at Anfield to regain the lead and they stayed there. Wolves took over as the main challengers and hammered the Blues 7-0 at Molineux on 22nd February. They responded though with a ten match unbeaten run to take them to the brink of the title.

On 22nd April Everton lost 2-0 at Charlton, but Wolves could only draw 0-0 at Bolton meaning the Blues were five points clear with two games left.

Tommy Lawton had been a pivotal figure in the side, scoring 34 goals in 38 appearances while Alex Stevenson and Torry Gillick also got double figures. The key to success was a settled first eleven which picked itself when fit.

The following September, Britain declared war on Germany, meaning the Football League did not resume until 1946. By this time, the title winning players best days were behind them.

1940
BOMB
DAMAGE

During World War Two, Goodison Park was damaged by air raids that were carried out by German bombers over the city of Liverpool.

The ground's proximity to the city's docks meant it was not surprising that it was hit on 18th September 1940. The Gwladys Street stand was most affected, with damage being caused to an outer wall, water pipes and the electricity supply.

Another bomb dropped in a schoolyard causing damage to the walls of the Bullens Road stand. A third bomb destroyed hoardings that surrounded the club's practice ground. Other bombs that night fell on Walton prison and a nurses' home in Fazakerley.

The repairs at Goodison Park, which cost £5,000, were carried out by Messrs Leitch and paid for by the War Damages Commission. If you look closely today, splinter damage is still visible in the brickwork of the Gwladys Street stand.

During World War Two, five players who had appeared for Everton are known to have been killed whilst on active service. The most prominent of these was Thomas Robson of the RAF Volunteer Reserve, who played 29 times in 1929-30.

1948
RECORD
ATTENDANCE

On 18th September 1948 Goodison Park recorded its highest ever attendance when a crowd of 78,299 watched the Merseyside Derby.

The evening papers reported a number of injuries to fans, caused largely by the swaying of the crowd. The first half was a tight affair, with Liverpool having the best chance when Billy Liddell's shot was tipped around the post by Ted Sagar.

In the second half Everton lost Tommy Jones though injury and Liverpool made their advantage count with ten minutes remaining. Liddell passed to Willie Fagan whose powerful shot gave Sagar no chance.

With six minutes to go Everton had a corner that was only half cleared by the Reds defence. Walter Boyes hit an angled shot goalwards which beat the keeper and was then handled on the line by a defender.

Ephraim Dodds stepped up to take the penalty and although Cyril Sidlow got a hand to the ball, he couldn't keep it out of the net. Despite both sides trying hard for the rest of the game neither could find a winner.

The next two season's derbies attracted crowds of 70,812 and 71,150. In 1962-63 the first derby for eleven years also saw a 70,000-plus crowd, but gradual capacity reductions since mean attendances are now little more than half that record figure.

1951
RELEGATED ON
GOAL AVERAGE

Everton were relegated for only the second time
in their history in 1950-51, when the bottom three
teams all finished with the same number of points.

The Blues won only two of their first eleven
games. They rarely looked like avoiding the drop
apart from brief upturn in form in December, when
they picked up nine out of a possible ten points.
At the beginning of March a 2-0 defeat at Bolton
was the start of a nine match winless run in which
Everton scored only two goals.

On 28th April the Blues won 1-0 at Derby in
their penultimate game, meaning their fate was in
their own hands. They were now third from bottom,
two points clear of the relegation zone occupied by
Chelsea and Sheffield Wednesday.

Everton's final game was away to Wednesday,
while Chelsea faced Bolton at home. A draw would
be keep Everton up and they could even afford to
lose providing Chelsea failed to win.

At Hillsborough on 5th May Everton were
a shambles, with nerves completely getting the
better of them. They were 3-0 down at halftime
and eventually lost 6-0. At Stamford Bridge Chelsea
beat Bolton 4-0, meaning they climbed above
Everton on goal average and it would be the Blues
who joined Wednesday in the Second Division.

1953
TED SAGAR
LEAVES

Goalkeeper Ted Sagar, the oldest player to appear for Everton, left the club in 1953 after an astonishing 24 years there.

Sagar joined Everton as a teenager in March 1929 and became the first choice keeper in 1931-32. That season Everton were crowned champions and he played in all but one of the league games. He remained the club's first choice keeper up until

the outbreak of World War Two, winning a second league title in 1938-39.

When the Football League resumed in 1946-47 Sagar was again Everton's number one and remained so until 1950-51, when they were relegated. Sagar remained for two more years as a back-up, making his last appearance away to Plymouth on 15th November 1952 at the age of 42 years and 282 days.

At the end of 1952-53 Sagar's playing contract was not renewed and although a position was offered on the coaching staff he opted to run a pub instead. As a parting gift, he was presented with £1,000 in reward for 24 years unbroken service.

He made a total of 495 appearances for Everton and was capped four times by England. He was the club's record appearance holder until he was overtaken by Neville Southall in the 1990s.

1953
SECOND DIVISION
SEMI-FINALISTS

Everton missed out on promotion in 1952-53 but enjoyed a run to the semi-finals of the FA Cup, where they almost completed one of the greatest ever comebacks.

Dave Hickson came of age during the cup run, scoring three goals in the early rounds. These included the winner against Manchester United in the fifth round, watched by 77,920 at Goodison Park.

The bulk of the 70,000 in attendance at Maine Road for the semi-final against Bolton were Evertonians. However the Blues were outclassed in the first half, during which Hickson had to go off for fifteen minutes with a head injury. Nat Lofthouse scored two and created another as Bolton stormed into a 4-0 lead after 41 minutes.

Shortly before halftime Everton were awarded a penalty but Tommy Clinton hit his kick wide. A minute into the second half John Parker pulled one back for the Blues, then Peter Farrell made it 4-2 from a free kick after 77 minutes.

With eight minutes to go Parker scored his second of the game and the impossible was beginning to look probable. For the remainder of the game Everton besieged the Bolton goal but they could not find the equaliser that would have forced a replay.

1954
BACK TO THE
FIRST DIVISION

Everton won promotion back to the top flight in 1953-54, but it was much tighter at the top of the table than it had been 23 years earlier.

A 3-0 win over Rotherham on 13th March was Everton's fourth in succession and took them to the top of the table with nine games left. However the Blues were still only two points clear of Leicester in third place. They then won just one of their next seven, meaning they still needed maximum points from their last two games to be sure of going up.

The penultimate game of the season saw Birmingham beaten 4-0 at Goodison Park. On 29th April, the Blues travelled to Oldham for a rearranged fixture, knowing anything less than victory would see Blackburn go up in their place. They made no mistake, leading 4-0 at halftime thanks to two goals from John Parker and others from Thomas Jones and Dave Hickson.

Leicester finished as champions on goal average and Everton went up in second place with Blackburn finishing just one point behind them. It had been a far more nerve-wracking season than 1930-31 when the Blues had finished ten points ahead of the third placed team.

1957
THE
FLOODLIT CUP

Floodlights were first installed at Goodison Park in 1957, the same year as at Anfield. To celebrate the switch on and the 75th anniversary of the Liverpool County FA, Everton and Liverpool played each other home and away for the Floodlit Cup.

The County FA donated a silver trophy for the winners of the two-legged affair. As well as the general interest of seeing games under lights, there was further excitement as the two clubs were in separate divisions at the time. This led to plenty of pre-match build up in the local press.

Goodison's floodlights were the tallest in the country at the time and extremely powerful. There was a crowd of 58,771 for the first leg on 9th October, in which Eddie Thomas scored twice to give Everton a 2-0 win.

Three weeks later at Anfield there were 46,000 present and Everton were 3-0 down within 25 minutes. Dave Hickson's header shortly before halftime levelled the aggregate score. Then in the second half Jimmy Harris scored with ten minutes to give the Blues a 4-3 victory over the two legs.

The Floodlit Cup continued for another four years but was discontinued in 1962 when Liverpool were promoted back to the First Division.

1958
UNDERSOIL
HEATING

In 1958 Everton became the first English club to install undersoil heating to combat frozen pitches in winter.

Once the 1957-58 season had ended, over thirty miles of electric cables were laid six inches below the pitch by the Merseyside and North Wales Electricity Board. These were automated and would heat up as soon as the temperature dropped to a certain level.

The system was so good though that the drainage couldn't cope. For too many games the pitch was in poor condition due to excess water and large areas of slush. It was decided at the end of the 1959-60 season to rip the system out and only install another one when drainage improvements had been made.

After the extremely harsh winter of 1963, Everton put undersoil heating in again but this was not as effective as the first version. It was taken out in 1967, but in the early 1970s the club again reverted back to it, this time using hot water pipes rather than wires.

Nowadays, Premier League rules state that precautions must be taken against inclement weather. However this does not necessarily have to be by way of undersoil heating.

1958
HAT-TRICK AND
ON LOSING SIDE

Jimmy Harris scored a hat-trick for Everton against Tottenham Hotspur at White Hart Lane on 11th October 1958. However he still wasn't on the winning side as the Blues lost by the amazing score line of 10-4.

Alfie Stokes opened the scoring for Tottenham after just two minutes but eight minutes later Jimmy Harris equalised. There was then what the *Daily Mirror* described as an avalanche as Spurs scored five times to lead 6-1 at halftime.

Seven minutes into the second half Harris scored his second but on the hour Spurs scored again to lead 7-2. There were no further goals for twenty minutes, but the last eight minutes were frantic with the ball hitting the back of the net five times.

Harris completed his hat-trick then Bobby Smith got his fourth of the game to make it 9-3. Bobby Collins pulled another back for Everton before John Ryden scored to take Spurs to double figures.

Everton had not actually played too badly, but Spurs were rampant with their players eager to please new manager Bill Nicholson.

The hat-trick was the only one Harris got for Everton. In 1960 he left the club for Birmingham City, having scored 72 goals in 207 appearances, many of them on the right wing.

1959
OUTRAGE ON BOTH
SIDES AT TRANSFER

In December 1959 there was anger on both sides of Stanley Park when Dave Hickson was transferred from Everton to Liverpool.

Hickson had made his Everton debut at Leeds in September 1951. He became a regular in the side in 1952-53, being a star of that season's FA Cup run. The following season he scored 25 goals as the Blues were promoted back to the First Division.

In 1955 Hickson was sold to Aston Villa and from there moved to Huddersfield. After failing to settle at both clubs, he was back at Everton in 1957. Although he was not as prolific with his goal scoring form, he had still got a respectable six from twelve games so far that season before the move came about.

Evertonians were outraged that Hickson had been transferred to Liverpool, whose fans did not want a cast off. Two goals on his debut helped win them around and he later played for Tranmere Rovers, making him the only player to appear for Merseyside's top three clubs.

After his retirement, Hickson made it clear Everton was his main club and he went on to work at Goodison Park as a matchday host and tour guide prior to his death in 2013.

1960
THE GOLDEN
VISION

In November 1960 Everton signed one of the finest players ever to wear the royal blue shirt when Alex Young joined from Heart of Midlothian.

Young had already won two league titles north of the border and moved south along with George Thomson. Young formed a great goal scoring partnership with Roy Vernon when Everton won the Championship in 1963. He netted 22 times himself as well as having a hand in many others.

The Golden Vision was a phrase coined by Tottenham captain Danny Blanchflower. It referred to Young's ability to stroke the ball rather than kick it. He would glide past defenders and play precision passes, gaining adulation from fans who worshipped him. His status was emphasised when he was once left out of the side for a game at Blackpool to give Joe Royle an opportunity, leading to manager Harry Catterick being confronted by fans in the car park.

Young helped Everton to FA Cup success in 1966 and when two years later Ken Loach directed a drama about the relationship between the club and fans, he entitled it *The Golden Vision*.

Young played 275 times for Everton before leaving in 1968 to become manager of Glentoran. He has retained legendary status at the club, with another film, *Alex the Great*, being commissioned by his biographer Dr David France in 2016.

Everton manager Johnny Carey was infamously sacked in the back of a London taxi in 1961 after two and a half years in charge.

Carey was a Dubliner who captained Manchester United and then gained a reputation for youth development during four years as manager of Blackburn Rovers. After a poor start to 1958-59 Everton boss Ian Buchan was relieved of his duties and Carey appointed in his place. He promised attacking football, saying only the goalkeeper stopped the ball.

Everton finished sixteenth in 1958-59 and fifteenth the following season. His side was playing entertaining football, but conceded goals too easily. 1960-61 was much improved but Everton still lost too many games that they should have won.

Things came to a head on 14th April when Everton were fourth in the league with two games left. Carey and chairman John Moores travelled to London for an FA meeting and with speculation rife over his future, the manager demanded clarification. Moores suggested they take a taxi to a hotel and when pressed by Carey during the journey, the chairman responded by saying he was being replaced.

Despite the shock news, Carey still took charge of the team the following day for a 5-1 win over Cardiff. He then resigned and was replaced by Harry Catterick, who guided the club to great success.

1962
INTER CITIES
FAIRS CUP

Everton's first venture into European competition saw them knocked out in the first stage without even making it across the English Channel.

By finishing fourth in 1961-62 Everton entered the Inter Cities Fairs Cup, a forerunner of the UEFA Cup and Europa League. In the first round they were drawn against Scottish side Dunfermline Athletic, managed by Jock Stein who would later have great success with Celtic.

The first leg at Goodison Park on 24th October attracted a crowd of 40,224, which although respectable, was still lower than any of the seven league games so far that season. A bad tempered game saw several brawls and five players booked. It was settled by a 25th minute goal by Dennis Stevens, giving the Blues a slender lead to take into the second leg.

A week later at East End Park Everton fell behind to a sixth minute goal. The Blues then struggled to break down Dunfermline, who were deploying a sweeper at the back, an innovation at the time.

With two minutes to go, Everton were caught out by a long clearance to Harry Melrose, who toe poked the ball past Gordon West. Despite appeals for offside the goal stood and Everton's European adventure was over before it had begun.

1963
HARRY CATTERICK'S
FIRST TITLE

The first of Harry Catterick's two Football League Championships was in 1962-63, when Everton were unbeaten at Goodison Park all season.

The Blues won six out of their first seven games and were rarely off the top all season. At home they were unbeatable, winning fourteen and drawing seven of their 21 games.

With Roy Vernon and Alex Young in great goal scoring form crowds flocked through the turnstiles. The average over the season was 51,469 and the attendance topped 60,000 on five occasions.

A terrible winter meant Everton went seven weeks without a game at one stage due to postponements. They wobbled in March, losing twice in four days. However a 2-0 win at Aston Villa on 1st April was the first of a twelve match unbeaten run that took them clear of nearest challengers Tottenham and Burnley.

The title was secured on the last day of the season in front of 60,578 fans. Everton needed a win against Fulham to guarantee the championship. Roy Vernon scored twice within the first ten minutes and although Fulham got one back, Alex Scott restored the two goal advantage after half an hour. Vernon completed his hat-trick with seven minutes left to confirm Everton as champions for a sixth time.

1964
CHAMPIONS HAMMERED
AT ANFIELD

On 19th September 1964 Everton won at Anfield for the first time since 1951, stunning the champions with a 4-0 win.

Despite being 1963-64 league champions the season after Everton's success, Liverpool had endured a stuttering start to the 1964-65 season defending their title and were near the bottom, while Everton were in eighth. Despite there being some optimism for victory, nobody could foresee just how comprehensive it would end up being.

Everton were ahead in the first minute when Derek Temple seized on a poor clearance to hammer an unstoppable shot into the net from a tight angle. Just a minute later Liverpool were almost level but Roger Hunt's header bounced back off the bar.

Fred Pickering doubled Everton's lead after 35 minutes when a bobbling shot deceived Liverpool keeper Tommy Lawrence and trickled over the line. Three minutes before halftime, Colin Harvey made it 3-0 with a great finish after chesting the ball down.

Early in the second half Liverpool fought back. A Hunt effort glanced the bar and Jimmy Gabriel cleared a Peter Thompson shot off the line. However after 64 minutes Johnny Morrissey scored the fourth with a magnificent drive, ending any Liverpool hopes of a comeback.

The score line remains Everton's biggest post-war victory at Anfield.

1965
THE FIRST
SUBSTITUTE

FACT 49

On 28th August 1965 Everton used a substitute for the first time when John Hurst replaced the injured Fred Pickering.

Substitutes had been introduced at the beginning of the season but could only be used to replace injured players; meaning for the opening two games Everton's starting eleven remained unchanged.

In the 78th minute of Everton's game at Stoke City, Pickering got injured whilst scoring in the 1-1 draw. This led to eighteen-year-old Hurst coming of the bench for the remainder of the game.

On 12th October that year, Andy Rankin became Everton's first substitute at Goodison Park, as well as the first replacement keeper, when he came on for the injured Gordon West in a Fairs Cup tie with Nuremberg. Almost a year to the day after Hurst made history, Sandy Brown became Everton's first goal scoring substitute, getting the third goal in a 3-1 win over Liverpool.

In 1967-68 Hurst became a regular in the side and was an ever present in the title winning 1969-70 season. Although he was a defender, he wore the number ten shirt. He went on to make a total of 404 appearances for the club, with just sixteen of those as substitute.

1966
AN UNLIKELY FA
CUP FINAL HERO

When Everton won the FA Cup in dramatic circumstances in 1965-66, the match winner was a surprise inclusion in the starting line-up.

For the big game against Sheffield Wednesday on 14th May, manager Harry Catterick made the brave decision to leave out Fred Pickering. He was replaced by Mike Trebilcock, who had played only eight times for the Blues.

Wednesday took the lead after four minutes thanks to a cruel deflected goal off Ray Wilson. Alex Young then had a goal disallowed and a penalty appeal turned down before halftime. In the 57th minute Wednesday went further ahead when Gordon West could only parry a shot into the path of David Ford who made no mistake.

Just two minutes later Trebilcock scored from twelve yards to give Everton hope. Within five minutes he had scored again, hammering the ball home from the edge of the area after a free kick was poorly cleared.

With sixteen minutes left Everton completed the turnaround when Derek Temple seized on a miscontrolled ball to race clear and score. Trebilcock almost got his hat-trick in the last few minutes but was denied by keeper Ron Springett.

Everton had become the first club to come back from 2-0 to win the FA Cup, a feat no other club matched until Arsenal in 2014.

1966
THE
WORLD CUP

Goodison Park staged five games during the 1966 World Cup, hosting some of the world's best players and one of tournaments all time greatest matches.

Holders Brazil played all three of their group games at Goodison. In the first they beat Bulgaria 2-0 thanks to goals from Garrincha and the legendary Pele. Pele was injured for the next game which they lost 3-1 to Hungary, inspired by future European Footballer of the Year Florin Albert.

Pele returned for the group decider, but Brazil were beaten 3-1 by a Eusebio inspired Portugal, who progressed along with Hungary.

Goodison's quarter-final saw Portugal take on giant killers North Korea, who had stunned Italy in their group match at Middlesbrough's Ayresome Park. Against Portugal the Koreans raced into a 3-0 lead within 25 minutes, but Eusebio scored twice before halftime. He levelled on the hour then scored another penalty three minutes later. Jose Augosto made it 5-3 ten minutes from time to end Korea's dream.

The semi-final between West Germany and the USSR attracted the lowest attendance (38,000) of Goodison's five games. It was a physical battle which West Germany won 2-1, the crucial second goal coming from Franz Beckenbauer. When England next hosted a major tournament, Goodison was overlooked as a venue with Anfield being selected instead for Euro 96.

1966
FIRST £100,000+
TRANSFER

In the summer of 1966 Everton became the first British club to pay a six-figure transfer fee when they signed World Cup winner Alan Ball.

21-year-old Ball had been a member of England's World Cup winning side that summer. In order to persuade Blackpool to sell him though, Everton had to part with £110,000 to bring him to Goodison.

Ball scored the only goal on his debut at Fulham on 20th August. A week later, he endeared himself even further when he netted twice as the Blues beat Liverpool 3-1 at Goodison Park.

That 1966-67 season Ball was Everton's top scorer with eighteen goals. He could pass with precision, tackle with ferocity and had boundless energy. In 1969-70 he had an outstanding campaign as Everton won the title.

In December 1971, with Ball 26 years old, the previous season's Double winners Arsenal made a British record transfer offer of £220,000. He was not seeking a move and Everton did not want to sell, but the fee was too good to turn down. He had played a total of 251 times for Everton, scoring 79 goals.

After Arsenal, Ball played for Southampton, Blackpool and Bristol Rovers, retiring in 1984 aged 39. He died in 2007 of a heart attack, aged just 61.

1967
MORE THAN 100,000
WATCH CUP TIE

FACT 53

When Everton beat Liverpool in the fifth round of the FA Cup on 13th February 1967, over 100,000 fans watched the game on both sides of Stanley Park.

Everton were the cup holders and Liverpool the league champions, so it was the tie everybody wanted to see. To cope with the overwhelming demand for a game played at 7pm on a Saturday giant screens were erected so 40,000 fans could watch the game at Anfield.

There were 65,000 fans inside Goodison Park but the match itself was not a classic. It was played in a swirling gale and there were no more than half a dozen chances throughout the game.

The decisive goal came just before halftime when Alan Ball seized on a poor back pass by Gordon Milne. Showing great opportunism he scored with a half volley from just outside the six-yard box.

Liverpool were the better side in the second half but Everton's defence was firm. The Reds resorted to pumping high balls into the Everton box which were dealt with easily and the local press reported that they had "refused to crack". Despite this triumph, Everton's run was over in the next round when they were beaten by Nottingham Forest.

1968
FIRST COLOUR
FA CUP FINAL

Everton appeared in the first FA Cup final to be televised in colour, but ended up on the losing side after an extra time goal.

The Blues had knocked out Southport, Carlisle, Tranmere, Leicester and Leeds on their way to Wembley. They were favourites for the final against West Bromwich Albion, having finished above them in the league and won both home and away fixtures during the season.

Both teams wore their away strips for the game, Everton's being yellow shirts with blue shorts. It was a disappointing event, with neither side showing their usual attacking flair. The two defences were solid and the midfielders cancelled each other out. Chances were few and far between. Everton's best was five minutes from time but Jimmy Husband headed over the bar with the keeper stranded.

After a goalless ninety minutes a replay at Hillsborough in Sheffield looked inevitable. However three minutes into extra time Jeff Astle seized on a momentary lapse of concentration to fire the ball through a gap in the defence.

Everton could not find an equaliser and it would be sixteen more years before they were back at Wembley for an FA Cup final.

1970
CATTERICK'S
SECOND TITLE

Everton won their seventh Football League Championship in 1969-70, as Harry Catterick's School of Science enjoyed their finest moment.

There are no definitive origins of the School of Science term — it goes back as far as the 1920s. However if an Everton team epitomised it, it was Catterick's second title winning side.

The Blues were unstoppable at the start of the season, winning eleven out of their first thirteen games. The midfield trio of Howard Kendall, Alan Ball and Colin Harvey played attractive football and up front Alan Whittle was in devastating form.

Apart from brief periods in September and January, Everton were top of the table all season. Leeds United were the only side who looked capable of overhauling them but they were distracted by runs to the semi-finals of both the FA and European Cups.

Everton hit form at just the right time, being unbeaten in their last fourteen games. Particularly satisfying during this run was a 2-0 win over Liverpool at Anfield.

The title was secured on 1st April in the third from last game. Goals from Harvey and Whittle were enough to beat West Bromwich Albion 2-0 at Goodison Park in front of 58,523 fans, the highest crowd of the season. The Blues went on to finish the season with 66 points, just one short of the First Division record.

1970
THE FIRST PENALTIES
IN EUROPEAN CUP

On 4th November 1970 Everton were involved in the European Cup's first penalty shoot-out, beating Borussia Monchengladbach 4-3 at Goodison Park.

After a 1-1 draw in West Germany, Johnny Morrissey gave Everton a first minute lead in the return leg. However Herbert Laumen levelled before halftime and there was no further scoring. In previous years a replay at a neutral venue or coin toss had been used to settle drawn ties, but UEFA had now agreed to go along with penalty shoot-outs, admitting they still weren't ideal.

Everton's Joe Royle took the first kick and saw his effort saved, before Klauss Sieloff scored for Borussia. Alan Ball then hit the target and Laumen missed meaning it was all square after two kicks each.

Both sides converted their third and fourth kicks, Morrissey and Howard Kendall being Everton's scorers. Sandy Brown then netted the fifth kick, meaning Ludwig Muller had to score to keep Borussia in the tie. To the delight of the home crowd Andy Rankin saved his effort and Everton were through to the quarterfinal.

The following March Everton faced Greek side Panathinaikos and went out on away goals, drawing 1-1 at home then 0-0 in Athens. It would be 44 years before they had another crack at Europe's premier club competition.

1971
A TRUE ONE
CLUB MAN

Brian Labone, who made more outfield appearances for Everton than anyone else, played his last game for the club in 1971.

Labone was seventeen years old when he joined the Blues in the summer of 1957. He made his debut at the age of eighteen and went on to become a dominant figure in central defence, making a total of 534 appearances and scoring twice. He was a good reader of the game, strong and good in the air. His only weakness was his left foot.

A League Championship winner in 1963, Labone then captained the side to FA Cup success in 1966 and another title in 1970. He famously observed that "one Evertonian is worth twenty Liverpudlians" and was capped 26 times by England. Throughout his career he was booked only once and a great tribute was paid to him by eighties skipper Kevin Ratcliffe who said that if there was a team of Everton captains, it was Labone who would lead them out.

Labone was forced to retire from playing after sustaining an Achilles tendon injury, but he continued to work for the club in a commercial capacity. He died in tragic circumstances in 2006, collapsing near his home after attending an Everton fans function.

Everton's biggest league victory since World War Two was on 28th November 1971 when they thrashed Southampton 8-0, causing the scoreboard to run out of space.

On a snowy afternoon David Johnson opened the scoring in the thirteenth minute with an angled shot. Three minutes later Joe Royle added a second after collecting an Alan Whittle pass. Johnson got the third after half an hour and in the fortieth minute Royle headed in a Howard Kendall cross.

On the stroke of halftime Alan Ball ran half the length of the pitch and slid the ball past keeper Eric Martin. After an hour, Royle completed his hat-trick with a superb half volley from the edge of the box.

Royle scored with a glancing header after 72 minutes for his fourth and Everton's seventh. With five minutes left, Johnson got a headed goal for his own hat-trick and finally end Southampton's misery.

The score line was so big that the Goodison Park scoreboard didn't have enough room for all of the scorers. Instead, they listed the order of goals by the player's shirt number rather than their name. That evening's *Football Echo* headline was "Royle Record in Everton Avalanche".

Everton first played on a Sunday in 1974, when the government eased restrictions due to a power shortage.

At that time the thought of football matches being played on a Sunday was unthinkable. However an energy crisis meant that the government and football authorities allowed Sunday games to ease pressure on the National Grid on Saturdays.

Many clubs weren't keen but Everton decided to give it a go and rescheduled their FA Cup fourth round tie with West Bromwich Albion to Sunday 27th January. To get round a law that barred the charging of admission to sporting events on Sundays, entrance was free providing fans purchased a team sheet. Coincidentally these were priced at the usual admission cost for whatever part of the ground they were on sale.

53,509 fans turned out for the tie, 20,000 more than had attended the previous round. It finished 0-0 and three days later Second Division Albion won the replay 1-0 at The Hawthorns. That game was played in the afternoon so that the floodlights didn't have to be used.

With the energy crisis over by March, it would be ten more seasons before Everton would play on a Sunday again, with the onset of live televised football.

After twelve years as manager, during which he won two titles and the FA Cup, Harry Catterick was persuaded to take up another position within the club in April 1973.

Catterick was appointed after the infamous sacking of Johnny Carey in a London taxi. Within two years he had delivered the league title, doing so by making some astute signings to go alongside the big name buys. He also instilled a strict sense of discipline amongst the players.

Catterick tried to avoid the media and wouldn't allow players to give interviews. He also wasn't happy when Everton games were televised as it allowed the opposition to view their tactics.

After winning the FA Cup in 1966, Everton reached the final in 1968 but were beaten by West Bromwich Albion. By now Catterick was developing a second great team, with the likes of Joe Royle, Howard Kendall and Alan Ball establishing themselves. They recovered from losing the cup final to win the league in 1970.

In January 1972 Catterick suffered a heart attack at a time when Everton were already struggling after the sale of Alan Ball to Arsenal. In April the following year the Blues were fifteenth in the table when Catterick was relieved of his duties by the board. He became general manager with Billy Bingham coming in as manager.

1977
LEAGUE CUP
AGONY

In 1977 Everton were beaten in the only English cup final that required two replays to determine the winners.

Victories over Cambridge United, Stockport County, Coventry City, Manchester United and Bolton Wanderers took Everton to their first League Cup final, where they faced Aston Villa at Wembley on 12th March 1977.

The match was an anti-climatic and dull 0-0 draw. Four days later at Hillsborough in Sheffield, an early goal appeared to have given Villa victory. However Bob Latchford equalised for the Blues in the last minute and there were no further goals, meaning a second replay at Old Trafford was necessary.

The deciding game was not until four weeks later and it was confirmed beforehand that penalties would settle the matter if necessary. Latchford scored for Everton in the 38th minute and the game really came to life in four frantic second half minutes towards the end. Chris Nicholl and Brian Little scored to give Villa the lead but Mick Lyons then equalised for Everton to force extra time.

Just as penalties looked inevitable, Evertonians hearts were broken two minutes before the end when Terry Darracott misjudged a cross and Little smashed the ball home to seal victory for Villa.

1978
BOB LATCHFORD'S
THIRTY GOALS

Everton centre forward Bob Latchford earned himself a newspaper prize in 1977-78 by scoring thirty league goals.

This was a period where Liverpool were dominating on Merseyside, but Latchford was a player who gave Evertonians some pride. Signed from Birmingham in 1974, he was strong in the air, could shoot with both feet and had an uncanny ability to get himself into dangerous positions.

For the 1977-78 season the *Daily Express* offered £10,000 to any player who could hit thirty league goals, something that had not been done for six years. With three games to go Latchford was on 28, but he failed to score in a 0-0 draw at Middlesbrough and 3-1 defeat at West Bromwich Albion.

On the last day of the season Everton led Chelsea 3-0 after an hour at Goodison Park, but Latchford hadn't got on the scoresheet. In the 72nd minute he got his first of the afternoon with a header, then Mike Lyons made it 5-0. In the 78th minute Everton were awarded a penalty, which Latchford dispatched to hit the thirty mark.

Although Latchford was given what was a huge sum of money for a footballer at the time, he didn't keep all of it for himself. He shared it out among team-mates and club staff, leaving him with just £200.

1978
FACT 63
MATCHWINNER TOLD TO GET OFF PITCH

Andy King was a derby hero on 28th October 1978 when he gave Everton their first victory over Liverpool for seven years. At the end of the game though he was told to get off the pitch by a police officer.

The Blues had endured a miserable derby run since beating the Reds in November 1971 and hadn't won in thirteen league games.

Going into this fixture at Goodison Park, Everton were second in the table, four points behind Liverpool. They needed a victory to demonstrate they could be serious title challengers.

Everton had the better of an all action first half, Bob Latchford going agonisingly close when he looped a header over the keeper only for the ball to bounce just wide of the post.

In the 59th minute Andy King scored with an unstoppable shot from the edge of the penalty

area. In a hectic last half hour, George Wood made crucial saves from Kenny Dalglish and Graeme Souness, while for the Blues Geoff Nulty shot wide after seizing on a poor defensive clearance.

Deafening roars greeted the final whistle. However as fans celebrated and King was interviewed by a television reporter, a police officer wasn't happy and told King to get off the pitch. Before King could even respond, the officer had pushed him off altogether.

1979
GOAL ON ONLY APPEARANCE

Teenager Ross Jack scored on his one and only appearance for Everton in 1979.

Jack was sixteen years old when he joined Everton from Highland League side Ross County in 1975. As a forward, opportunities were limited with players such as Bob Latchford and Andy King ahead of him.

An opportunity arose when King was unavailable for the midweek trip to Middlesbrough on 6th March 1979, two weeks before Jack's twentieth birthday. Jack wore the number seven shirt and opened the scoring after half an hour. Fourteen minutes into the second half Latchford extended Everton's lead and Boro pulled one back with a late David Armstrong penalty.

King was back in the side for the next game and Jack had a loan spell at Cardiff. In December that year he was sold to Norwich City for £20,000 and later played for Lincoln City and a number of clubs in Scotland.

Since 2014 Jack has been manager of part-time Turriff United in the Highland League. He also works for the Scottish Football Association as a development officer in the Highland region.

1980
KEVIN
RATCLIFFE

The most successful captain in Everton's history made his debut for the club in 1980.

Kevin Ratcliffe joined as an apprentice in 1977 and was nineteen when he made his debut at Manchester United on 12th March 1980. He was impressive in a 0-0 draw but did not establish himself as a regular until midway through the 1982-83 season.

In 1983-84 Ratcliffe became captain and that season he became the youngest skipper to lift the FA Cup since Bobby Moore in 1964. Over the next three years he lifted the League Championship trophy twice as well as the European Cup Winners Cup.

Ratcliffe had electric pace and an ability to read the game and anticipate problems. This more than made up for the fact his actual ball playing ability was not as good as others in the team. He scored only twice in 459 games for the club, one of them a tame 25 yard effort in the Anfield derby that Liverpool keeper Bruce Grobbelaar somehow allowed to slip from his grasp.

In 1992 Ratcliffe left the club and had a brief spell with Dundee in Scotland, then came back to the English league and played for Cardiff, Derby and Chester City. He was also capped 59 times by Wales and now works on the after dinner speaking circuit.

1981
IMRE VARADI'S
CELEBRATORY PIE

Imre Varadi scored the decisive goal in an FA Cup
fourth round derby over Liverpool in 1981, then had
a pie thrown in his face.

A Londoner of Hungarian descent, Varadi
was nineteen years old when he joined Everton
from Sheffield United in 1979. Over the next two
seasons he played 35 times and scored seven goals,
with the highlight undoubtedly being his goal against
the Reds.

Liverpool were third in the league and
Everton tenth, but form counts for little in derbies
and Peter Eastoe put Everton ahead after a quarter
of an hour.

After an hour Eamonn O'Keefe crossed and
Varadi managed to steer the ball past Ray Clemence
from a tight angle. He celebrated by running behind
the goal towards the Park End terrace, not realising
that was where Liverpool's fans were gathered and
a pie was thrown in his face. Jimmy Case pulled one
back for Liverpool but Everton held on for victory,
with Varadi missing a couple more chances.

Varadi was sold by incoming manager Howard
Kendall at the end of the season. He is still a
regular visitor to Goodison and is reminded every
time about the pie, which he says was meat and
potato and that he can still taste it.

1981
LEE OUT,
KENDALL IN

After finishing just clear of the relegation zone two seasons running, Gordon Lee was sacked at the end of 1980-81 and replaced by former player Howard Kendall.

Lee had taken over from Billy Bingham in January 1977, getting to that season's League Cup final. He then led the Blues to third and fourth place finishes in the next two seasons.

In 1979-80 Everton reached the semi-final of the FA Cup, losing to West Ham after a replay. However in the league they finished nineteenth, just one place and four points above the relegation zone. The following season they were fifteenth, but this time they beat he drop by only three points.

Lee was sacked at the end of the season and replaced by Howard Kendall. During his time at Everton, Lee had given opportunities to two players who would be instrumental in the success of the 1980s, Kevin Ratcliffe and Graeme Sharp.

For two years Everton struggled under Kendall, but things suddenly clicked into place in the middle of the 1983-84 season. By combining experience with younger players who had a point to prove and experience, the Blues were finally a side to be feared again. They then entered the most trophy-laden period of their history.

1982
MICK
LYONS

Mick Lyons, one of the most committed players to play for Everton, left the club in 1982.

A boyhood Evertonian, Lyons came through the junior ranks as a centre forward. However with competition from David Johnson in that department, he was converted to a defender. He made his debut at Nottingham Forest on 20th March 1971, wearing the number six shirt and scoring in a 3-2 defeat.

The 1970s were not the best years to be an Evertonian, but the continuing presence of Lyons, who became captain, was one shining light. He was strong in the air, not afraid of a tackle and also useful as an emergency centre forward. He would often move into attack in the closing stages of games when Everton were losing and in 1973-74 was even the club's leading scorer with nine goals. Four decades on, players are still encouraged to 'do a Mick Lyons' at Everton games.

Lyons earned Under-23 and B caps for England, but a call up to the full squad eluded him. He left for Sheffield Wednesday in 1982 after losing his place to Billy Wright. He had scored 59 goals in 473 appearances and returned in a coaching capacity at the end of the decade.

A player who would prove to be one of the most important signings of the decade joined Everton in November 1983.

Andy Gray had signed for Wolves in an English record £1.5 million deal in 1979 and scored the winning goal as they won the League Cup in 1980. They were relegated in 1982 but Gray remained with them when they started the following season in the Second Division.

Howard Kendall gambled on signing Gray, who had been troubled by knee injuries, for just £250,000. By the end of the season he was a Wembley hero, heading Everton's second goal in the FA Cup final against Watford.

In 1984-85 Gray was not first choice at the start of the season, but an injury to Adrian Heath allowed him a run in the side where he formed an effective partnership with Graeme Sharp. After winning a league title winners medal, he scored one of the goals as Everton beat Rapid Vienna in Rotterdam to win the European Cup Winners Cup.

Gray was a courageous player, not afraid to go in to situations irrespective of the risk of injury. Fans loved his fearless approach and were sorry to see him leave the club for Aston Villa in the summer of 1985 following the arrival of Gary Lineker.

1984
ALL MERSEYSIDE
LEAGUE CUP FINAL

The turnaround in Everton's fortunes in the 1980s began with a run to the League Cup final, where they were desperately unlucky not to beat Liverpool at Wembley.

Victories over Chesterfield, West Ham and Coventry took Everton to the quarterfinal, where they were drawn away to Third Division Oxford United. The Blues trailed 1-0 before a poorly hit back pass let in Adrian Heath to equalise.

After winning the replay 4-1, Everton beat Aston Villa in the semi-final to set up an all Merseyside encounter at Wembley. On 25th March 100,000 Reds and Blues travelled own together and stood side by side in the stadium, a lesson to the rest of the county in days when hooliganism at games was rife.

The game was a dour one, but in the first half Liverpool defender Alan Hansen appeared to clear Adrian Heath's goal bound shot with his hand. No penalty was given to the dismay of Evertonians in the stadium. The match finished 0-0 and afterwards, both sets of players did a joint lap of honour.

Three days later at Maine Road in Manchester the replay was another dull game, with Reds' captain Graeme Souness's first half strike being the only goal. In both games though Everton had equipped themselves well and good times were just around the corner.

1984
FA CUP
WINNERS

Everton made up for their League Cup disappointment by lifting the FA Cup, beating Watford 2-0 in the final at Wembley.

After beating Stoke 1-0 away from home in the third round, Everton needed two replays to get past Gillingham of the Third Division. Wins over Shrewsbury and Notts County set up a semi-final with Southampton.

At Arsenal's Highbury Stadium Adrian Heath scored the only goal in extra time to take Everton to their first FA Cup final in sixteen years. They then went into the final in good form, winning four and drawing two of their last six league games.

Early in the game John Barnes had a great opportunity to give Watford the lead but he miscued his shot with only Neville Southall to beat. Mo Johnston then went close with a header but Everton then took control. Graeme Sharp headed wide and Kevin Richardson's shot his the side netting.

After 38 minutes, Sharp broke the deadlock when he turned a pass from Gary Stevens into the net. Six minutes after halftime a header from Andy Gray extended Everton's lead and Watford never looked like getting back into the game.

The victory was Everton's fourth FA Cup triumph and it signalled the start of the most successful period in their history.

1984
SHARPY'S DERBY
GOAL OF THE SEASON

72

On Everton 20th October 1984 won at Anfield for the first time since 1970, with Graeme Sharp's stunning volley being voted BBC *Match of the Day's* goal of the season.

Everton had lost only one of their last eight going into this fixture. The Blues had triumphed over their great rivals in the Charity Shield but they knew it would be a far bigger test at Anfield.

Everton bossed the game from start to finish, with Peter Reid dominant in midfield, exploiting every Liverpool weakness. Gary Stevens was particularly assured at the back and Neville Southall a steady pair of hands in goal.

Sharp's match winning goal came in the 48th minute, when he controlled the ball, swivelled and unleashed an unstoppable volley over Bruce Grobbelaar into the net.

At the end of the game the celebrations among players and supporters were long as Everton celebrated beating the European champions in their own stadium to move up to fourth in the table. This victory gave Everton the belief that they could build on their FA Cup success.

Later that season, with the league title already secured, Everton completed a double over Liverpool, winning the return 1-0 at Goodison. *Match of the Day* viewers also voted Sharp's Anfield strike the best goal of the season.

1985
THE
CHAMPIONS

After a slow start to the 1984-85 season, Everton picked up and stormed to their first league title in fifteen years.

The Blues lost their first two games but then went six unbeaten. The October victory at Anfield increased confidence further and started a run of five straight wins without conceding a goal.

Everton went top of the league for the first time with a 3-0 win over Leicester at the beginning of November. They remained there until the week before Christmas when a 4-3 home defeat to Chelsea saw then drop to second below Tottenham.

A 2-1 win at Sunderland on Boxing Day was the start of an incredible sequence of results that saw Everton surge ahead of their rivals and claim the title with five games to spare, picking up fifty of 54 points available.

The title was secured on the first Bank Holiday Monday in May when 50,514 packed Goodison Park to see the Blues beat QPR 2-0.

Everton had the luxury of being able to lose three of their last five games and still finish thirteen points ahead of their nearest rivals. Sadly they were never able to test themselves against Europe's elite, as English clubs were then banned from UEFA competitions following the actions of Liverpool fans at the Heysel Stadium disaster.

1985 EUROPEAN GLORY

Everton's only European trophy to date came in 1984-85 when they won the European Cup Winners Cup on a memorable night in Rotterdam.

Straightforward victories over University College Dublin, Inter Bratislava and Fortuna Sittard took the Blues to the semi-final, where they were drawn with heavyweights Bayern Munich.

In front of 67,000 fans at the Olympic Stadium, Everton silenced the crowd and earned a 0-0 draw. Back at Goodison Park though, a 38th minute goal from Dieter Hoeness left the Blues with a mountain to climb. However, in one of the most exciting 45 minutes of football ever seen at Goodison, second half goals from Graeme Sharp, Andy Gray and Trevor Steven took Everton to the final.

The Blues were overwhelming favourites to defeat Rapid Vienna who were happy to sit back and soak up the pressure. The first half was frustrating and in the 39th minute a Gray goal was ruled out for offside.

The breakthrough finally came in the 57th minute, Gray scoring after being set up by Sharp. Steven got the second in the 73rd minute to put Everton in total control and although Hans Krankl scored for Rapid with five minutes left, Kevin Sheedy got a third for the Blues. Everton's fans, who made up most of the crowd, partied long into the night.

1986
DOUBLE
DISAPPOINTMENT

Everton came so close to glory in 1985-86 but ended the season empty handed as they finished runners up to Liverpool in both the First Division and FA Cup.

Manchester United started off the season with ten straight wins but by New Year they had been pegged back by the Blues and Liverpool, as well as surprise challengers Chelsea and West Ham.

On 22nd February goals from Kevin Ratcliffe and Gary Lineker gave Everton a 2-0 win over Liverpool at Anfield. This stretched the Blues' lead over the Reds to eight points with twelve games remaining. However by the end of the league season Everton had been overhauled as Liverpool took 31 points out of a possible 33.

A week after the league season ended, Everton faced Liverpool at Wembley in the first all Merseyside FA Cup final. Supporters again journeyed to the game together and stood next to each other on the terraces. Gary Lineker's 27th minute goal put Everton ahead at the interval, but in the second half Liverpool scored three times to complete the Double and leave the Blues dejected.

1986
GARY
LINEKER

In his only season at Everton Gary Lineker scored forty goals in all competitions, the highest total of any Everton player since World War Two.

Everton paid Leicester City £800,000 for Lineker, who had been the First Division's joint top scorer with 24 goals in 1984-85. He was a player who could combine speed with the ability to concert chances with clinical precision.

Lineker's contribution was immense in a season in which Everton were so near yet so far from glory. He played in 41 of the 42 league games, scoring thirty goals. This included three hat-tricks and he scored ten times in other competitions to take his total to forty.

At the end of the season Lineker won both Professional Footballers Association and Football Writers Player of the Year awards. In that summer's World Cup in Mexico he was the tournament's top scorer with six goals.

Everton's ability to hold onto Lineker was hindered by the European ban. When Barcelona came in with a £2.6 million bid, it was impossible to turn down. Lineker went on to enjoy a successful career both on the pitch and in the media. He continues to say that the Everton side of 1985-86 was the best he ever played in.

In 1986-87 Everton overcame the loss of Gary Lineker to regain the Football League Championship trophy from Liverpool.

The money raised from Gary Lineker's sale wasn't spent on one big name replacement. Instead veteran defender Paul Power came in alongside midfielders Kevin Langley and Neal Adams.

At the start of the season Everton were without some key players though injury including Peter Reid, Pat Van Den Hauwe and Neville Southall. In the first half of the season they drew too many games and going into the Christmas fixtures they were fourth in the table.

A 3-0 win over Wimbledon at Goodison Park on 20th December was the first of six straight wins that took the Blues up to second. At the end of January they were two points behind leaders Arsenal but with a game in hand. Everton then won seven games in succession in March and April to take them to the brink of glory.

There was a historic opportunity to virtually clinch the title at Anfield on 25th April but the Blues lost 3-1. On 4th May, Van Den Hauwe's goal at Norwich confirmed them as champions with two games still to go. Some Everton historians feel it was Howard Kendall's greatest managerial achievement due to the difficulties faced.

1987
FOURTH SUCCESSIVE
CHARITY SHIELD

Everton are the only side to win the Charity Shield (now Community Shield) four seasons running, achieving the feat between 1984 and 1987.

Everton's FA Cup win in 1984 qualified them for the annual season curtain raiser for the first time since 1970. Their opponents at Wembley were Liverpool and the Blues won thanks to a 55th minute own goal by Reds keeper Bruce Grobbelaar. Graeme Sharp's shot was cleared by Alan Hansen, only for the ball to bounce back off Grobbelaar into the net.

The following year Everton were back at Wembley as champions and faced Manchester United, their conquerors in the FA Cup final. Goals from Trevor Steven and Adrian Heath gave the Blues victory in Gary Lineker's first game for the club.

In 1986 Everton took part after finishing runners up to Liverpool in both the First Division and FA Cup. Heath put the Blues ahead in the eightieth minute, but Ian Rush equalised with two minutes remaining. As was customary then, the shield was held by both clubs for six months each.

After winning the league again in 1987, Everton faced surprise FA Cup winners Coventry that year. Wayne Clarke's 44th minute goal was enough to win the game and keep the shield at Goodison for a fourth year, something no other club has ever achieved.

Tony Cottee joined Everton in a British record transfer in August 1988. He made the perfect start but failed to live up to the heights expected in his six years at the club.

Everton paid £2.2 million to West Ham United for the striker at the beginning of August. It was a record at the time but the fee was surpassed at the end of the month when Ian Rush re-joined Liverpool from Juventus.

Cottee made his debut for the Blues against Newcastle at Goodison Park on 27th August. He opened the scoring after just 34 seconds and went on to score a hat-trick in a 4-0 victory.

Over the next six seasons Cottee played 205 games for Everton, scoring 99 goals. It seemed a respectable enough return, but the club didn't challenge at the top of the table following his arrival. Cottee had joined an Everton side that was hoping to regain the title from Liverpool, but left one that had only just avoided relegation.

Cottee's Everton career was frustrating partly due to injury hit campaigns and also due to him never developing a regular strike partner. In 1994 he rejoined West Ham in a deal that brought David Burrows to Everton.

1988
LOWEST
CROWD

The lowest crowd to watch a competitive match at Goodison Park was on 20th December 1988, when just 3,703 saw Everton beat Millwall in the Simod Cup.

Simod were that season's sponsors of the Full Members Cup, a competition inaugurated in 1985 for clubs in the top two divisions of the Football League. Even the prospect of a Wembley final didn't generate interest for fans, who saw it as a pointless regurgitation of the FA and League Cups.

Unlike the other bigger clubs, Everton continued to enter but crowds were always low. With fans also having to find money for two league home games over Christmas this third round tie, Everton's first of the competition that season, was always one to miss.

Squad rotation was rare at the time but Colin Harvey made six changes to the side that started the previous weekend's game at QPR. A goal from Tony Cottee and an own goal from Terry Hurlock took Everton into the next round.

Further victories over Wimbledon and QPR meant Everton reached the final, where they were beaten 4-3 after extra time by Nottingham Forest at a half full Wembley.

Everton also reached the final in 1991, when it was known as The Zenith Data Systems Cup, losing to Crystal Palace. The competition was discontinued after 1992.

1989
SECOND ALL MERSEYSIDE
FA CUP FINAL

In 1989 Everton and Liverpool played each other in the FA cup final for the second time in four years. That season's competition though was overshadowed by the Hillsborough disaster just five weeks before.

On the day Everton beat Norwich 1-0 at Villa Park in the semi-final, 96 Liverpool fans were crushed to death due to severe overcrowding at Hillsborough in Sheffield. After much deliberation the club decided to continue in the competition and beat Nottingham Forest in the replayed game to set up a final with Everton at Wembley.

The final was just five weeks after Hillsborough, with both teams wearing black armbands and a one-minute silence taking place beforehand. John Aldridge scored for the Reds after four minutes and this looked to have been enough until Stuart McCall equalised for the Blues with the last kick of the game.

Ian Rush restored Liverpool's lead five minutes into extra time but seven minutes later McCall scored with a brilliant volley. Just before the teams changed ends, Rush scored again and there were no further goals as Everton found themselves on the losing side against Liverpool in a final again.

1990
HOWARD KENDALL'S
MARRIAGE

When Howard Kendall returned for his second spell as manager of Everton in 1990 he described his relationship with the club as a marriage.

Kendall left the Blues after winning the title for a second time in 1987. He led Athletic Bilbao to UEFA Cup qualification but he was always hindered by the club policy of only signing Basque players. After being sacked in November 1989, he returned to England the following month as manager of Manchester City.

When Colin Harvey was sacked by Everton at the beginning of November 1990, they were in the relegation zone. Kendall's City side were in fifth place but he agreed to return to Goodison Park. He justified the move to confused City fans by saying that their club was a love affair for him, but Everton was a marriage.

Kendall reinstated Harvey as his assistant. In his first season back at Everton he steered them to safety, finishing ninth, but he was unable to restore the glory days of the 1980s. After two mid table finishes, he resigned in December 1993 after the board refused funds for new signings.

1991
THE GREATEST
CUP TIE EVER

The FA Cup fifth round replay between Everton and Liverpool at Goodison Park on 20th February 1991, when Everton came from behind four times, has been dubbed the greatest cup-tie ever by many pundits.

Everton trailed 1-0 at halftime to a Peter Beardsley goal, but the introduction of Stuart McCall for the second half made them more effective in midfield. Within two minutes of the restart Graeme Sharp had headed an equaliser, then Pat Nevin fired over the bar with only the keeper to beat.

Beardsley restored Liverpool's lead in the seventieth minute but Sharp equalised again three minutes later, poking the ball into the net after two Reds players collided. Everton were only level for four minutes however as an Ian Rush header made it 3-2.

With five minutes left Howard Kendall sent on Tony Cottee and Pat Nevin. Cottee had to wait until the last minute for his first touch but it was a vital one as he scored to force extra time.

A curling effort from John Barnes put Liverpool 4-3 ahead but with just a minute remaining, Cottee seized on more calamitous defending to equalise. A week later the sides met at Goodison Park again. Everton won a much less intense game 1-0 but they then went out at West Ham in the next round.

1991
TOP POST WAR
GOALSCORER LEAVES

Graeme Sharp, Everton's leading scorer since World War Two, left the club in October 1991.

Everton paid Dumbarton just £180,000 for Sharp in 1980 and he spent the next decade playing alongside Everton greats such as Andy Gray, Gary Lineker and Adrian Heath.

Sharp's role as a second striker rather than target man meant his goals per game ratio was less than others, but he made up for this with what he could create. He had strength in the air, wonderful control and ability to battle his way out of tight positions.

Amongst Sharp's most memorable goals are the opening goal in the 1984 FA Cup final and a strike against Liverpool in October that year which earned a first victory at Anfield since 1970. Later in the 1984-85 season, he scored the equalising goal against Bayern Munich in the memorable European Cup Winners Cup semi-final.

By the time Sharp moved to newly promoted Oldham in 1991, he had scored 150 goals in 412 appearances, more than any other post war Everton player. He now works for the media in Merseyside and is a club ambassador.

1992
THE PREMIER
LEAGUE

Everton were one of just three clubs who had been Football League founder members that also featured in the inaugural season of the Premier League.

For 1992-93 the top flight clubs became part of a financial new set up that kept all television revenues for themselves, rather than share them with lower division clubs. Of the 22 clubs that competed in the first Premier League season, only Aston Villa and Blackburn Rovers had been founder members of the Football League back in 1888.

Everton had a decent start to the season, avoiding defeat in their first five games. These included an impressive 3-0 win over Manchester United at Old Trafford. Things took a downward turn though with just one win in nine.

There was a boost in early December with a 2-1 derby win over Liverpool at Goodison Park, the first league win over the Reds since 1988. This wasn't a springboard however and Everton lost their next league game 1-0 at Sheffield United.

Every time it looked like a corner had been turned, things got worse. Three straight wins in January were followed by four defeats in a row. Everton eventually finished in thirteenth place, their lowest position since 1983.

1994
THE
GREAT ESCAPE

Everton continued to struggle in 1993-94 and only escaped relegation on a dramatic last day of the season at Goodison Park.

Again the Blues started well, winning their first three games only to lose their next three. There was a morale boosting 2-0 derby win over Liverpool at Goodison Park, but they then lost 5-1 at home to Norwich.

After just 13,667 saw Everton beat Southampton 1-0 at home in early December, only the second league win in ten games, Howard Kendall resigned. He was replaced by Mike Walker, who had challenged for the title with unfancied Norwich the previous season.

Walker was unable to arrest the slide and Everton fell from thirteenth to twentieth. Going into the final day of the season, any two out of six teams could still go down, but crucially Everton's fate was out of their hands.

After half an hour Wimbledon led 2-0 at Goodison, but the Blues got a lifeline thanks to a Graham Stuart penalty. In the second half a Barry Horne screamer made it 2-2 and with nine minutes to go Stuart's bobbling shot crept into the net. With Oldham and Sheffield United both losing, Everton had stayed up and there were tears of joy on the pitch afterwards from players and fans alike.

1994
JOE ROYLE'S
DOGS OF WAR

When Joe Royle became manager of Everton in November 1994 he instituted a playing style known as the Dogs of War to get the Blues out of trouble.

Everton had the worst start to a season in their history, failing to win any of their first twelve games. A 1-0 win over West Ham in their thirteenth game was still unlucky for Mike Walker, who was sacked and replaced by Royle, a former midfield favourite for the Blues.

Royle got off to the perfect start, beating Liverpool 2-0 in his first game. This was the start of three successive wins that lifted Everton from the bottom of the table to one place outside the relegation zone.

The key to the improved form was greater resilience in the centre of the pitch. Andy Hinchcliffe was the only flair player of Royle's preferred midfield line-up alongside Joe Parkinson, John Ebbrell and Barry Horne.

The phrase 'Dogs of War' was coined unintentionally by Royle but it stuck over the next two seasons. In 1994-95 Everton eventually finished fifteenth out of 22 teams and won the FA Cup. The following season they finished sixth, their first top half placing since 1992.

1995
FA CUP
TRIUMPH

A season that began with the worst start in Everton's history ended with an FA Cup triumph at Wembley.

The Blues reached the semi-final without conceding a goal, beating Derby, Bristol City, Norwich and Newcastle. They then stunned Tottenham at Elland Road, winning 4-1.

For the final on 20th May Manchester United, who a week earlier had lost out on the title, were the pre match favourites. Everton suffered a blow when Duncan Ferguson failed to recover from a hernia operation in time and had to be content with a place on the bench. However United were without the influential Andy Cole and Eric Cantona.

It was a tough opening with the referee letting a lot of hard tackles go. After half an hour Everton took the lead when Paul Rideout headed in after Graham Stuart had hit the bar. Rather than sit back the Blues took the game to United for the rest of the half, Stuart having an effort well saved by Peter Schmeichel.

For the second half United sent on Ryan Giggs for defender Steve Bruce who was struggling with injury. Everton had more defending to do than the first half but generally kept United at bay. Late in the game Neville Southall made a great double save to deny Mark Hughes and ensure Everton had won a fifth FA Cup.

1997
NEVILLE SOUTHALL
LEAVES

Goalkeeper Neville Southall, Everton's record appearance holder, left the club in November 1997.

Southall joined Everton from Bury in 1981 but didn't establish himself as the club's first choice keeper until 1983-84. In the championship season of 1984-85 he made some stunning saves, including tipping a header over the bar in the last minute as Everton beat closest challengers Tottenham. At the end of the season he was voted the Football Writers Player of the Year.

Many blame an injury Southall picked up on international duty for Wales as the reason Everton failed to win the league or cup in 1985-86. When he returned in the November of the following season,

he helped Everton win the title.

Southall was a perfectionist and often stayed behind for extra training. When Everton won the FA Cup in 1995, he was the only surviving member of the 1984 winning side. Although an ever present in 1995-96, Southall faced competition from Paul Gerrard the following season. In November 1997 Thomas Mhyre arrived, leading to Southall going out on loan to Southend and then Stoke for the remainder of the season.

Southall last appeared for Everton in a 2-0 home defeat to Tottenham on 29th November 1997. It was his 750th appearance for the club in all competitions, a record unlikely to ever be broken.

1998
ANOTHER
ESCAPE

For the second time in five seasons, Everton avoided the drop on the last day of the campaign in 1997-98.

After the resignation of Joe Royle, Howard Kendall returned to Everton in August 1997 for a third spell in charge.

The season was played against a backdrop of financial problems. Everton were bottom of the table at the end of November but a run of just two defeats in twelve games lifted them up to sixteenth.

Too many games were being drawn and the Blues failed to pull away to safety. A 4-0 defeat at Arsenal in their penultimate game saw them drop back into the bottom three. This meant that they had to beat Coventry at Goodison Park on the final day of the season and hope that Bolton failed to win at Chelsea.

Gareth Farrelly scored an early goal for Everton but they couldn't finish the game off, Nick Barmby missing a penalty. At Stamford Bridge, Bolton held out until the 73rd minute before falling behind.

With a minute to go, Dion Dublin equalised for Coventry to stun the Goodison crowd. There was relief all round when Chelsea scored a second, meaning Everton had stayed up due to having a better goal difference. A few weeks later, Kendall left the club by mutual consent.

2002
DAVID
MOYES

In March 2002 Everton appointed a manager who reversed the struggles of recent seasons and turned them into regular challengers for a European place.

After one league win in thirteen games took Everton close to the relegation zone, Walter Smith was sacked. Moyes, who had just missed out on promotion to the Premier League with Preston, was appointed and won his first two games to help restore confidence. They eventually finished in fifteenth; seven points clear of the bottom three.

The following season Everton finished seventh, their first top half finish since 1996. Although 2003-04 was a disappointment, he was given more time and finished fourth in 2004-05.

Despite not having the spending power of the so-called bigger clubs, Moyes took Everton into Europe on four occasions. He also steered them to the FA Cup final and two semi-finals, in the FA and League Cups.

During Moyes's eleven years in charge only Arsene Wenger and Sir Alex Ferguson were in their posts longer. Goodison Park became a place all teams feared visiting and they finished in the top eight in seven successive seasons.

Full recognition of Moyes's management abilities were confirmed that when the time came for him to leave Everton, it was to take over from Ferguson at Manchester United.

2002
WAYNE
ROONEY

In October 2002 Wayne Rooney burst onto
the scene. He became Everton's youngest ever
goalscorer, scoring in a League Cup tie and then hit
a late winner for his first Premier League strike.

Rooney was a schoolboy star of the FA Youth
Cup winning side in 2001-02 and was promoted to
the first team squad. He made his debut in the
opening game of 2002-03 against Tottenham at
Goodison Park.

On 1st October Rooney came off the bench
after an hour of a League Cup tie at Wrexham. The
Blues were already 1-0 up and in the 82nd minute
Rooney received a flick on from Duncan Ferguson
and drilled the ball into the net. With a minute to go
he scored again to complete a 3-0 victory. His goals
meant he had broken a seventy-year record that
had been held by Tommy Lawton.

On 19th October Rooney came on with ten
minutes remaining against Arsenal at Goodison Park.
It was 1-1 and in the final minute he scored with a
beautiful curling shot from outside the area, ending
the Gunners' thirty match unbeaten run.

Five days after that goal Rooney signed his
first professional contract and by the end of the
season he was an England international. He joined
Manchester United in 2004, but returned to
Everton thirteen years later.

2005
CHAMPIONS LEAGUE
QUALIFICATION

Everton defied the odds in 2004-05 and finished fourth in the table, securing a place in the qualifying rounds of the following season's Champions League.

After finishing only six points ahead of the relegation zone in 2003-04, Everton then had to cope with the loss of Wayne Rooney, who was sold to Manchester United.

Despite many pundits predicting a relegation battle, the Blues won seven out of their first ten games. A first league victory over Liverpool since 1999 on 11th December moved them up to second, just three points behind leaders Chelsea.

The summer signing of Australian international Tim Cahill had been an inspiring one and he went onto finish the season as top scorer with eleven goals.

In January out of contract midfielder Thomas Gravesen left for Real Madrid leading to the title challenge tailing off. Despite his departure, Everton responded with a statement of intent by signing James Beattie for a club record £6 million.

Everton held on to secure fourth place with victory over Newcastle at Goodison Park in the penultimate game of the season. The Blues ended the season three points ahead of Liverpool, the first time since 1987 they had finished above their great rivals.

2005
CHAMPIONS LEAGUE
HEARTBREAK

Everton's first venture into Europe's top competition since 1971 ended in disappointment when they were denied in controversial circumstances.

In the qualifying round Everton were un-seeded and were handed a tough task against Villareal of Spain. On 9th August at Goodison Park they began brightly but fell behind in the 27th minute. James Beattie equalised fifteen minutes later but Villareal scored again in first half injury time.

There was no further scoring leaving the Blues with a mountain to climb in Spain two weeks later. They trailed 1-0 at halftime but a 69th minute free kick from Mikel Arteta gave them hope.

With confidence growing, Tim Cahill's deflected cross bounced off the bar then Duncan Ferguson had a header brilliantly saved. From the corner, Ferguson appeared to have levelled the tie but the goal was ruled out for a foul by Darren Bent. Everton's hopes were then dashed in the last minute when Diego Forlan scored to give Villareal a 4-2 aggregate win.

Television replays later showed that it was actually Bent who had been fouled in the area. There was not even the consolation of a UEFA Cup run for Everton, as they were then eliminated at the first hurdle by Dinamo Bucharest 5-2 on aggregate.

FACT 95
JOSE BAXTER: EVERTON'S YOUNGEST PLAYER

Jose Baxter is the youngest ever player to appear for Everton He also holds the record as the youngest starter of a Premier League game.

Baxter joined Everton at the age of six and turned professional in the summer of 2008 on leaving school. In the opening game of 2008-09, at home to Blackburn Rovers on 16th August, he came on as a 78th minute substitute. This made him the club's youngest player aged just 16 years and 191

days. The score was 2-2 when he came on and he went close with a header, but Blackburn won the game thanks to an injury time winner.

The following week Baxter started Everton's game away to West Bromwich Albion, making him the Premier League's youngest ever starter. However his career failed to progress and over four seasons he made only fifteen appearances.

Baxter was released at the end of 2011-12 and joined Oldham Athletic. He went on to play For Sheffield United, but was banned for a year in 2016 after failing a drugs test. Everton did however give him an opportunity to resurrect his career and he rejoined the club in the under-23 set up for the 2017-18 season.

2009
THE FASTEST FA CUP
FINAL GOAL

Louis Saha scored the fastest ever FA Cup final goal in 2009 but it was not enough to win the trophy for Everton.

Everton were drawn against Premier League opposition in each round from the fourth onwards. Their route to Wembley included victory over local rivals Liverpool in a fourth round replay and victory over Manchester United on penalties in the semi-final.

After just 25 seconds of the final, Saha scored with a magnificent strike after Marouane Fellaini had knocked the ball down to him. This rattled Chelsea but the Blues failed to capitalise and with 21 minutes gone Didier Drogba headed an equaliser.

Chelsea were on top for the rest of the first half but at the break David Moyes replaced Tony Hibbert with Lars Jacobsen, allowing Tim Cahill to get further forward. Saha had a header go just inches over the bar as the game remained wide open for twenty minutes.

After 71 minutes Frank Lampard evaded the challenge of Phil Neville to score with a great effort. Chelsea took control and soon after Florent Malouda fired over then had a shot that appeared to bounce off the bar over the line but no goal was given. Despite those let-offs Everton could not find a way back into the game and endured a record eighth final defeat.

2013
FIRST OVERSEAS
MANAGER

When David Moyes left at the end of 2012-13 to take on the Manchester United job, Everton appointed their first manager from outside the British Isles.

Roberto Martinez was in charge of the Wigan side that had knocked the Blues out of the FA Cup on their way to winning the trophy in 2013. Although Wigan were also relegated the Catalonian had a reputation for playing attractive football and coping with limited budgets and sales of key players.

In 2013-14 Martinez led Everton to a fifth place finish and their total of 72 points was their highest ever in a Premier League season. His approach was a refreshing one, especially against the so-called bigger clubs, against whom he was not prepared to defend and try holding out for a draw.

In 2014-15 however Everton never got over a pre season that was hindered by players returning late from the World Cup. They finished eleventh in the league and also went out of both cups at the first stage.

2015-16 was also disappointing. Although Everton reached the semi-finals of both cup competitions, they again struggled in the league. They were in twelfth place and with protests being planned for the last game, the decision was taken to dismiss Martinez to spare embarrassment.

2013
VICTORY AT
OLD TRAFFORD

Everton ended a 21-year wait for a victory against Manchester United at Old Trafford, heaping more misery on former manager David Moyes on 4th December 2013.

Moyes had been given a rousing send off when he left Everton at the end of 2012-13 to take on the United job. However relations had soured in the summer when he pursued Marouane Fellaini, who he did sign, and Leighton Baines, who remained at Goodison. Moyes had angered Evertonians by suggesting the club should allow the players to further their careers.

In an entertaining game United hit the bar twice and Kevin Mirallas also struck the woodwork from a free kick. The Blues refused to be intimidated by United's big names, with Phil Jagielka and James McCarthy putting in outstanding performances.

With four minutes remaining, Brian Oviedo drilled in a low shot after a cross from Romelu Lukaku. It secured a first victory for Everton at Old Trafford since August 1992 and kept them in fifth place, while champions United were down in ninth.

Later in the season, United were beaten 2-0 by Everton on Moyes's first return to Goodison Park. It was a result that brought his short spell as United boss to an end as he was sacked two days later.

2015
EUROPA LEAGUE
GOLDEN BOOT

Everton's 2014-15 Europa League campaign ended in a disappointing defeat in the round of sixteen but striker Romelu Lukaku did finish as the competition's joint top scorer.

Everton went straight into the group stages and finished top of their group, ahead of Wolfsburg, Lille and Krasnodar. In the round of 32 they were paired with Swiss side Young Boys Berne. They fell behind to an early goal in the away leg but came back to cruise to a 4-1 victory, Lukaku netting his first Everton hat-trick. In the return at Goodison Park, Lukaku was twice on target as Everton completed the job with a 3-1 win.

The round of sixteen saw a tough tie with Ukrainians Dinamo Kiev, with Everton securing a narrow 2-1 win in the home leg thanks to a late Lukaku penalty. By the time of the second leg, Champions League defeats for other teams meant Everton were the last English club in Europe.

In Kiev's Olympic Stadium, Everton were trailing 2-0 when Lukaku scored after half an hour to level the tie. However they eventually lost 5-2, going out 6-4 on aggregate.

Lukaku's seven goals in the two knockout ties had taken his tally to eight in the competition, making him the joint winner of its *Golden Boot* along with Brazilian Alan of Red Bull Salzburg.

2017
RECORD TRANSFERS
& BIG SAM

During the 2017 transfer window Everton broke their record for both the incoming and outgoing transfer fees. However the new arrivals couldn't save manager Ronald Koeman from being dismissed.

By the time Romelu Lukaku joined Manchester United for £75 million on 10th July, Everton had already spent £87 million on seven players. Three of these, Davy Klaasen, Jordan Pickford and Michael Keane had cost more than £20 million.

Everton had also brought Wayne Rooney back to the club on a free transfer along with Cuco Martina and Boris Mathis. On 16th August, Everton broke their transfer record by paying Swansea £40 million for attacking midfielder Gylfi Sigurosson.

Despite all the new arrivals, Everton struggled and won only two of their first nine games. Koeman, who had been in charge little over year, was sacked after a 5-2 home defeat to Arsenal on 22nd October, which saw the Blues drop into the relegation zone.

Koeman was replaced by Sam Allardyce, who was taking charge of his seventh Premiership club. He steadied things and began with a seven game unbeaten run to steer the Blues away from danger.

The 100 Facts Series